Dream Haters
Tips for Young Dreamers on Achieving While Avoiding the Haters

Dream Haters
Tips for Young Dreamers on Achieving While Avoiding the Haters

by
Tera R. Reid

First Edition, First Printing

Contents

How Can You Ever Be a Failure if You Never Stop Trying?

Introduction

I wrote this book just for YOU. Yes, you! I know you are saying, "She doesn't know me." You're right, I probably don't know you. But, I do understand more about you than you think.

I know that you have a lot of dreams and goals for your future. I know that right now, you are struggling with some situations that can keep you from those goals, and you aren't quite sure how to get through it. You aren't really comfortable talking to a lot of people about your fears and you just wish someone would understand what you are facing without judging you and making you feel like you are wrong. Sound familiar? You're not alone. Just about everyone struggles with those same decisions and situations. It's not easy. To be honest, as you get older, the decisions get tougher. But the good thing is that as you get older, you also get wiser and better at making those hard choices.

I also know that sometimes adults can make you feel like your problems are not important, or they are just "kids' stuff." They tend to dismiss you and act like your issues are small. I agree that they can seem very judgmental and insensitive to your feelings. However, sometimes as people get older, they get the "been there, done that" mentality. It just means that they have already been through and conquered some of the very things you are experiencing right now. Those same concerns are no longer difficult for them because they have already mastered them. So, don't always think of them as dismissing you, they are just letting you know that you can get through these rough times just like they did. Once you learn how to navigate through the craziness of it all, you can keep moving so that you can get to your goals.

That is why I wrote this book. I wanted to help you find a way to reach your highest aspirations and dreams despite the obstacles that come your way.

Dreams:

Dreams live inside of all of us. It's a wonderful thing to be a dreamer. Dreams give you vision. Without a vision, you have nothing to look forward to or work towards. By allowing yourself to have a vision of what your life can be like, it gives you power and motivation to work towards your goals.

Sometimes our dreams are realistic, like going to college and becoming a doctor or an engineer. Some dreams are just an escape from reality, like growing up to become a superhero. While some dreams are just a fantasy, you should never give up on things that really are possible (even when you feel like it's impossible).

Some dreams we grow out of, or change our minds about. Then there are dreams that won't go away, they always stay with you. Those are the dreams you should focus on. Usually those very dreams are your key to a lifetime of happiness.

There are two kinds of dreams in life. Dreams that others control and dreams that you have control over. It is important to understand the difference in these dreams and how they affect your life.

Dreams that others control are dreams affected by another person's actions. It is important that you understand the Golden Rule of Dreams. I will repeat it many times throughout this book because it is so important to you succeeding in life. ***The only dream that you can control is yours***. So quit trying to force others to cooperate and live out your dreams. It will never work. While we can compromise and come to agreements with other people, there will also be times where we can't. It is then that you have to learn what is important to you reaching ***your*** dreams.

Dreams that you control surround your personal growth and destiny. Whether you believe it or not, you have power and control over your dreams. While there may be all kinds of haters and distractions in your way, ultimately, you are responsible for your own dreams.

There is nothing worse than someone who blames the fact that they did not reach their dreams on other people. While some circumstances may force us to alter some things in life, ultimately if you truly have a dream in your heart, you should not let any obstacle or excuse keep you from it.

So does working towards your dreams mean you are going to have to work hard? Will it mean giving up some fun things you would rather be doing to concentrate on your goals? Does it mean that you are going to have to let go of some friends? The answer to all these questions is YES! Anything worth having requires some sacrifice.

Dreams and Haters

I've always worked with young people as a profession. The majority of the young people I worked with got into trouble at school, home, or legally.   While society labeled them as "delinquent, troubled, or at risk"; I simply called them "my kids" because I cared about each and every one of them. I personally know that I have worked with some of the most remarkable young people in the world.   I also know that each and every one of them had a dream.

The problem was, not many people agreed with me about their talents and potential. Other people usually only saw the negative things about them.   I chose to see the positive side of them. I always took the time to see their talents and skills. I looked past the negative paper trail that followed them, and got to know who they really were.   I struggled hard against stereotypes and other obstacles to help them get the recognition they deserved.

However, I also had to struggle to help those young people understand that their reputation was ruining their future.

You may be in the same position and letting harmful things and judgments hold you back. Unfortunately, most people won't take the time to get to know who you really are. They definitely don't want to give you a second chance when you mess up. Society loves to judge and label others. However, judgments can be overcome. You must understand how your current actions are related to your future goals. Take the time to learn from each mistake and try not to repeat them. Heed the advice of wiser, older people who want to help you in your life. Those lessons may help you towards your goals.

I know adults are always in your ear telling you that you need to do this or do that for your future. But, they don't always understand the challenges you face in trying to get to your goals. They also usually just tell you what to do, and not how avoid the obstacles that come at you. How can you possibly do the right thing when you don't even know how to handle the situations you come across?

As you read this book, you will find family dreams, educational dreams, and life dreams. While it is impossible for me to list every life scenario; I tried to give you some of the typical issues that young people have shared with me over the years. As you get older, you will learn that life throws more curves at you than you ever imagined! Life is never going to be a straight road. Think about a map. It will take you straight to your destination, but it won't tell you about the detours and roadblocks along the way. Your life path is just like taking a road trip with a map. You may plot a straight course, but find that it is full of detours and alternate routes. It is important to understand that while you may have to take a different route sometimes, you can still get to your dreams.

While each dream I discuss may not be specifically related to you, I'm sure you can use some of the tips that go along with it. Each dream I talk about is how your ideal world looks. If everything in your life was going as you would like it to go, then this is how your life would look. It's the good life you dream about. It's the family, life path, etc. that you envision for yourself. It's the place you would love to be in.

Unfortunately, every dream has a hater. We all know what haters are. A hater is anyone or anything that doesn't want you to reach those dreams. Haters create drama, confusion, and chaos just to keep you from living in a peaceful world. I want you to know that regardless of what the haters look like in your life right now, you can still accomplish your dreams. Haters can be hard to overcome, but are not impossible.

I like to talk about haters because I look at them like fuel to a fire. Haters are what I use to keep moving throughout my life just to prove that I *can* when I've been told I *can't*. We live a world where anything is possible. That same world is full of a lot of people and perceptions who will spend time telling you that you can't. Those are haters. They are the people and things who spend a lot of time trying to convince you that you aren't good enough, attractive enough, smart enough, thin enough, etc. to aspire to your dreams. They are not who you should be listening to. If you have a dream, go for it!

Now, in no way am I saying that you should dream to win American Idol or Sunday Best if you can't sing. Remember, I did say realistic. However, you can work in the music industry if you know that music is your passion. Just find your own talents and let your skills lead you to your destiny.

In order to conquer the haters in your life, this book will give you tips to assist you in getting around the day to day drama. Now I don't claim to have all the answers. But, I do know that I have been happiest when I'm able to help people through their struggles. That is my purpose and dream.   I'm living mine by writing this book. Hopefully I can help you to find your purpose and dreams.

I have also included some quotes that you can think on from time to time. I often have been inspired by others who have been through their own struggles and opposition.   It helped me to realize that if they made it, I could too. A lot of those who inspired me have been able to turn around their circumstances. I recommend that you take some time to look up the story of certain celebrities, public figures, and even people you know.   There are a lot of things they endured to get to where they are now. Nobody starts at the top!

In addition to the tips and quotes, I've included a few activities that you may find helpful. They will help you focus on what things you need to do to reach your goals. They are simple written activities and guides designed to give you some help and direction as you navigate your path.

As you go through this journey of life I have to be honest and tell you that there will be hard times and you will wonder why you even bother trying. A lot of times in this book, I will give you some "tough love" not as a lecture, but as a way of pushing you to keep moving, especially when you don't feel like it. My hope is that I can help you work around some of those daily struggles you face so you can reach your aspirations. My biggest desire is that I can help you understand why you should never give up on your dreams!

Every situation in this book is about the dreams that you control. By the time you get to the end, you should be well aware of how to take control of your own dreams to make them reality. Now, I'm not claiming that this will be a "quick lifetime fix." A lot of topics in this book are things you will have to learn by trial and error. Many adults still struggle with the same issues, so I don't expect you to get it right every time, but I do want to give you an advantage. As you grow and mature, some things will get a lot easier, and some will still be difficult. The point is I want you to understand how to persevere to get to your goals.

Now, let's get busy! You've got dreams to reach!

The choice is yours to be angry, bitter, and unproductive, or to be happy, fulfilled, and successful in life.

Family Dreams

Regardless of how you define family; it's all love.

I can't begin to talk about your dreams without talking about your family. Your family plays a huge role in you accomplishing your dreams. They can be your biggest supporters and cheer you on to victory. Sometimes though, they can also be obstacles in the way of your goals.

Generally a family wants the best for their members, but sometimes they have strange ways of showing their true feelings. Honestly, some family members just don't know how to help you, so they may try to deter you to a path familiar to them. Others are afraid that if you don't succeed at first, that you will be devastated, so they try to avoid seeing you get hurt. Most family members love you and only want to see you reach your dreams. Keeping that in mind will help you even through the struggles and madness that can arise.

There are many ways to define a family. While the dictionary may give you standard definitions, I believe that family is what you make it. It is an ongoing relationship where love, support, and kindness is expected and received. In that same relationship you can feel misery, pain, and conflict. All of those emotions and many more are perfectly normal.

Families can take on many different forms. They can consist of any combination of mothers, fathers, sons, daughters, cousins, uncles, aunts, grandparents, etc. Family can also be those who have no blood relation such as in foster, adopted, or just people close to your family like your "play mama's and aunties." Regardless of how you define family, it's all love.

I wanted to start with family because that is always the beginning of our story. We all started somewhere; and regardless if you are with your biological family or adopted into one; it's all family and we belong somewhere. We have to deal with family and their habits on a regular basis. Some of those habits may be great, and some may get on your last nerve. As I talk about some of the dreams you have and the haters surrounding your family, I want you to know that regardless of what your family situation looks like right now, your goals are obtainable.

Dream: Having a peaceful family life

Hater: That one, two, or maybe ten relatives who always have some drama going on in and around the family.

Tip: Your family's issues do not have to define your future. Just because there is always some form of foolishness going on in and around your family does not mean you have to participate. The dramatic people in your family may even be the adults, but it still doesn't mean they are always right.

It takes all kinds of people to make the world go round. Guess what? All of those kinds of people are in your family. They may be people that you deal with on a daily basis, or relatives that you see every now and then. However, as long as there are families, there will be drama!

There can be a million reasons why drama exists in families. Sometimes different people are offended or hurt by others, and they lash out. There are also people in this world who are not happy with themselves. Because of this, they like to stir up drama among others just to make themselves feel important, or to make you as miserable as they are. These are just a few examples of the drama causing factors in families.

It is important for you to remember that you should not get caught up in the commotion. People involved in drama tend to end up doing and saying things that can't always be taken back. While you may be angry at the moment, you may find one day that you really do miss that sister or cousin you had the nasty words with. Once hurtful words come out your mouth, you can't take them back. You can apologize, but it's always there. You can change the course of a lifetime relationship in a few minutes. Is it really worth it? Think before you speak and act.

Now, you may say, it's easy for you. I bet you never had the drama I have in my family. Well, you may be right, but I will say that no family is drama free, even mine. So, while I may not be able to identify with your exact situation, I will say that I've had my share of drama. I'm sure I have relatives right now who have a problem with me for whatever reason. The difference is, I don't hold onto grudges. I still love those very family members, and will still talk to them and be there for them as much as I can.

Please be aware that I'm no fool. I know that some people you have to love from a distance. I'm not talking about physical, far away distance. I just mean that sometimes you can't keep certain people too close because they are too dramatic and always keep mess going. Those are the ones that you still love because they are family, but you love them far away from the drama. That keeps the drama from disrupting your life.

If you have a family member that you need to fix things with, do it now. Don't worry about who was wrong or try to be stubborn and hold onto petty things. Family is too important. Every day on this earth is a gift. Tomorrow is not promised to anyone. You really wouldn't want to tragically lose someone without them knowing how you really felt right? Let the pettiness go, and fix it NOW.

Dream: Desiring to break your negative family cycles

Hater: That one person who reminds you that all the women in your family got pregnant young and dropped out of school, and all the men were in and out of prison. Or everyone is a drunk, an addict, a drop out, etc… They seem to feel that you will be just like them.

Tip: Your genetics and heritage do not have to trap you. If you see negative cycles in your family or friends, then you need to make up in your mind how you plan on breaking those cycles. Don't let family members keep you from achieving your goals by expecting you to fall into the same negative patterns as they did. You should know that just because something happens from generation to generation does not necessarily make it a good tradition. However, it does mean it's easier to happen with you too. So, you need to develop a solid plan so that you can avoid falling into those same traps.

   If you have not already done so, today, write down your future plans. Write down 3 goals you have for yourself and 3 steps you can take to get there. By putting your plan into writing, you are making yourself more responsible and accountable. You can even cut out pictures to make a collage of what you envision for yourself, or write simple lines about what you will or will not be. (Example: "I will go to college, or I will not get pregnant (or get anyone pregnant) before I finish high school.") Once you've finished your goals, put them up in a spot that you will see them every day like on a mirror, in a notebook, etc. Every day, ask yourself, what have I done to work on my goals? If the answer is nothing, you are falling into the trap.

So, what if you already fell into the trap? It's never too late to turn it around. As long as you are still living, you have a chance to make it right. It may be harder, but it's not impossible. Get up and get busy. Write down your goals and the steps you need to get there. Try to find at least one or two people who can hold you accountable and help you to reach your dreams. Make sure that the people holding you accountable are responsible and are going to be serious about helping you reach your goals. If you don't know anyone who can hold you accountable, go find a local school, agency, church, etc. that can help you with your goals. Chances are you may find someone there who can help you get where you want to be.

Let's break those cycles! I believe in you. The question is, do you believe in yourself?

Dream Hater Activity 1

My Life Goals

3 goals for my life are:

_____

_____

_____

3 steps I can take to get there are:

_____

_____

_____

3 ways I can stay focused on the road to my goals

_____

_____

_____

People who can help me get to my goals:

_____

_____

Dream: Wishing your family were like_____

Hater: Wanting to be a part of the "perfect family" that lives across town.

Tip: Nobody has the luxury of picking the family they are born into. While your family may have their issues, remember that there is no such thing as a perfect family. Stop comparing yourself to others. You are only looking inside through a window. You don't see their whole lives. Think about it, on all the reality shows, how much drama and confusion goes on in the household? A lot. Now, imagine if you had cameras rolling on the perfect family. While they probably don't have as much "made for TV drama" as your favorite reality show, they also probably aren't as "perfect" as you think. For all you know, they may have total confusion going on in their house on a regular basis. Comparing yourself to others only makes things worse.

Be happy with the family God blessed you with. Biological or not. Forgive them for their mistakes. Most of the time, they are doing the best they know how to do. Even if they don't give their best, you can't let your anger at them keep you down. Understand that it is a problem on their part, not yours.

If you are able, try to sit down and talk with your family members. If you need a neutral party to help, ask a trusted person to mediate. If you family doesn't want to talk, don't worry. You did your part. Remember the golden rule of dreams; you can't control anyone but you! Keep moving forward, and don't let them hold you back.

If you don't have the opportunity to talk to your family or even know who they are, you can always form a family. Look at the circles you keep. Do you have any positive people in your life that you interact with on a regular basis? They may be the very people that God allowed into your life to help you through difficulties. Appreciate whatever form of a family you may have. They can make all the difference in the world. So, the choice is yours to be angry, bitter, and unproductive, *or* to be happy, fulfilled, and successful in life. Which would you rather have?

Dream: Wishing your parent didn't date or marry HIM or HER

Hater: The always present stepmother /stepfather or girlfriend/boyfriend of your parent that you really don't care for.

Tip: Believe it or not, parents are human too. Apart from taking care of you, they also may desire adult companionship as well. It's ok. They are entitled to happiness!! But, what if you really don't care for the person that your parent has chosen?

Your parent is in the relationship with that person, not you. So, remember that golden rule of dreaming. The only dreams you can control are yours. Your parents' dreams are your parents' business.

There are many reasons I find that young people don't like others dating their parents. Some teens are upset because ideally, they want their biological parents together. Or, it could be that they feel the person their parent has chosen is not good for them or doesn't treat them well. Sometimes, they just are jealous that their parent has interests outside of them. Whatever the reason, you have to deal with your emotions concerning the situation.

I'll give you an example. I worked with a teen that originally lived with his mother, but was sent to live with his father after he got into some trouble. Well, he would come to school daily upset saying how he didn't really like his father and stepmother because they ganged up on him all the time. He felt they treated his sister (their child) different and let her get away with things, but nagged him for no reason. He felt alone and criticized.

You may say, yeah, I know how he feels. Maybe you know that your parent has a bad relationship and you don't want them put in that situation. Or you may be saying, "they treat us (brothers and sisters) different than their own kids." It could be that you don't like them having a say about your discipline and consequences. Whatever the reason, I'm going to tell you how a mature person such as yourself handles this.

I recommend that you have a conversation with your parent, and express your true feelings. Be honest about how you feel. Your parents may not even be aware your feelings. Now ultimately what your parent chooses to do with their relationship is their business, not yours. Once you speak your peace (in a calm, respectful, non-threatening tone), then that's all you can do. The rest is up to them. Even if you feel you are right, all you can do is be there for your parent. Keep on loving them. Don't give them a hard time. They really need you. Remember, family is forever.

Bonus Tip: I want to add this tip because sometimes people mistreat and abuse others in relationships. If you observe this, or are a victim of abuse yourself, keep talking until someone believes you! Tell a teacher, family friend, law enforcement, or anyone who will listen until you get the help you need.

Dream: Achieving the goals that you choose

Hater: Your parents keep pushing you to become something different than you dream of being.

Tip: You don't have to agree with your parents all the time, but you should respect them. Your parents should know you quite well, and they may have valuable insight into what can help you be successful. The problem comes in when their dreams and your dreams for yourself don't line up.

You can't live out anyone else's dreams but yours. Now, your parents may have dreams of you becoming a doctor, but you want to live out your dream of being an artist. Your parents seem to feel that your art is just a hobby. However, you feel that it's your passion. They are always talking with you about the career and financial stability and benefits, but you have no interest in the medical field. How do you handle it?

When I was in middle school, I was interested in playing in the band. Actually, I wanted to play the saxophone. I thought it would be a cool instrument to learn. Well, on my class schedule I could only do one elective. I had a choice between band and a class called careers. My mom talked me into taking careers because she felt that it would help me in my future plans. (I think she just wanted me to think about working!) Anyway, I ended up taking careers, even though I thought I could have been a cool sax player. Now, I'm not saying she stopped a great saxophone player. Knowing me, I may have lost interest in it anyway. However, I never even gave her my reasons for wanting to play or even tried to speak up for myself. I just went along with her plans.

So, how do you handle this situation? You do your research. You start looking at possible careers you can have with your interests. You look at what the job outlook and the demand for the field looks like. You research required education, average salaries, and other options. Once you do some research, go back to your parents with your information. You can then have an educated line of reasoning regarding your choices. I'm still not saying that your parents will agree with you, but you will have impressed them with making an informed decision. You will have shown them that you are trying to be responsible for your future.

Remember it's just that, *your* future.

Dream: Not disappointing others

Hater: Regardless of how hard you try, you keep messing up.

Tip: Life is full of mistakes. You've made them in the past, and guess what? You will make more in the future. While mistakes are a natural part of life, if you seem to always make bad choices, it is possible that you may be a habitual poor decision maker. That means that you usually make the wrong choice in a situation.

So, let's talk about decisions. You have to learn to think of consequences before you act. You know the difference between right and wrong. Everything is a choice. So, when you are faced with a decision, you should ask yourself the five "W" questions: Who, What, When, Where, and Why?

Who is this going to involve or affect? Does this decision involve some shady people you know you really shouldn't be dealing with? Will participating in this potentially mess up your goals and dreams?

What is this going to involve? Will the decision involve you compromising your beliefs or morals? Is the activity legal?

When is this going to happen? Should you be at school during this time? Is this going to happen way past curfew? Is this happening the night before that big project is due?

Where is this taking place?   Is this the part of town I know I shouldn't be in? Is it over someone's house that I know I shouldn't be at?

Why am I doing it? Are you doing it because you are following someone else's lead? Is this something that you know your parents would not approve?

There are so many questions that can come out of the five "W's". You should be able to come up with your own questions just from a few of them when faced with challenging decisions.

So what if you try the five W's, and still screw up? I don't expect you to always make the right choice. Nobody does that. However, the more you think about your actions before you do them, the better chance you will have at getting it right. As you get older, if you continue to use this formula, you will make much better choices. Even when you don't always make the best decisions, don't be discouraged.   Difficulties in life can make you stronger if you handle them right. If you never fall or struggle, how will you ever be able to appreciate being on top?   So, are you going to dwell on that mistake, or are you going to keep trying to prove that you really are a worthy person who can do things the right way?   Wallowing in your pity just wastes time that you could be making things right. How can you ever be a disappointment if you never give up trying? So, get moving. You have goals to achieve, and as far as I know, nobody ever won by giving up!

You can't live out anyone's dreams but your own.

Dream: Wanting to be loved

Hater: You feel like your family/friends/or anyone else doesn't love you.

Tip: I know this is going to sound really lame, but I have to say it. You have to learn how to love yourself first. I'll tell you why. It's natural to expect love from others, especially your family. The problem is that if they don't return the love, you feel rejected and upset. You end up spending time looking for love from all the wrong people, and that will only make things worse. Even after you learn to develop a healthy love for yourself, any form of rejection you experience will still hurt. However, you can find the strength to go on and do your thing. Learning to love you is not an easy task, but it is possible. It takes time and lots of practice.

As humans, most people desire relationships with others. Those relationships can produce the love of family and friends, or even romantic love. Wanting love from others is natural, but if you don't receive it, don't let that derail your life and plans. When the time and person is right, you will get the love you desire. You may never get it from your family, but you may find a wonderful person one day who loves you just as if you were their family.

Until then, learn to love yourself. Oh, yeah, and understand what love really is. Don't fall for those claiming they love you as long as you do things for them their way. Real love doesn't require you doing things that compromise your values, safety, and judgment.

You know, this section is really important to me because I used to work with a few really special and talented young men and women. The problem was that while I saw how great they were, they could not see it for themselves. They had talents in music, dancing, writing, cosmetology, sports, etc. They had immense talent. When I asked them what they wanted to do with their lives, they would give me wonderful goals and plans. But they didn't believe in themselves. They would come show me their sketches, raps, hair styles they created, and just share so many of their talents with me. I would tell some of the young ladies that they were so pretty and special, but they didn't believe it themselves. I would tell some of the young men how talented and skilled they were, but they didn't believe it themselves. I may not have always verbally told them that I loved them, but I tried to show it in my actions. The problem was they didn't love themselves.

I would love to say that they learned to love themselves and became successful. But some of them haven't so far. While I never give up on anyone, I will say that they haven't learned yet how to believe in themselves. As a result, they have ended up on the streets, in prison, or have fallen into those traps I spoke of earlier. **If you don't believe in yourself, it doesn't matter how much others try to encourage you, you won't act on a belief you don't have.**

Try this exercise. Make sure you find one positive thing to say about yourself every single day. Today you may really like your hair. Or you may say that you are great at math. Whatever it is, find something positive to say about yourself and say it often. You can even write it down or make a collage that you look at when you are feeling sad. You will find that over time, you will have a lot more confidence and resilience than you thought was possible. Ok, now, I know you are rolling your eyes saying how lame that idea is. I know, I know, just try it!! I promise it really works!!

Now, be careful, I want you to love yourself, but I don't want you to be arrogant! There is a difference between being positive and being annoying! Once you learn how to properly love yourself without having a big head, you will also learn that you don't need others to validate you. You can do that for yourself! Try it, I dare you!

Dream Hater Activity 2

Positive Things About Me

I am good at:

People compliment me most on:

The feature/characteristic I like most about myself is:

I am a good person because:

Dream: Wishing you didn't fight with your parents all the time.

Hater: Like the old Fresh Prince and Jazzy Jeff song, "Parent's Just Don't Understand"

Tip: I know that you and your parents seem like you are from two different planets. They don't understand you. They don't listen to you. They criticize your friends, music, clothes, etc. Being a teen is tough because you aren't a baby, but you aren't an adult. You are expected to be responsible, but not given the freedom you want. (You're thinking, hey, she really does know me!) It's just another one of those, been there, done that situations.

When I was a teen, my mom and I had our fair share of mother/daughter battles. I felt that she was old fashioned and didn't understand the times and we just couldn't relate. I didn't understand why she would not let me participate in certain things or go certain places. She just worked my nerves sometimes!! (And now I realize that I worked hers too!) Sound familiar?

As an adult now, I have learned that some of the things I used to disagree with my mom about are things that I typically won't allow my own children to do. Why? Because I realized the value in what she taught me. It took me a while to get it, but I got it. She wanted me to be successful and she saw that certain choices I wanted to make were going to hinder that. I guess at this point you feel I'm just another adult trying to side with your parent. I'm not. Hear me out.

That been there, done that is reality. Sometimes your parents are hard on you not because they feel you are a baby, but because they want what's best for you. They want to see you reach your dreams. Sometimes they are hard on you because you aren't living up to your end. What do your grades look like? Are you always getting into trouble? Sometimes they are hard because they really don't understand you. That's when you learn to communicate!

How can you communicate with your parents? Find some uninterrupted time to discuss the things that bother you. Now when I say uninterrupted, don't try to talk when either of you is distracted or in a hurry. Chances are if you do it then, neither of you will really be listening. Once you find some one on one time, come to them in a respectful manner without the attitude, whining, and sarcasm. The mature way you approach them may make all the difference in them listening. Give them your reasons why you feel why you should be able to do certain things. Once you finish, listen to them with an open mind. Listen to their real reasons for not wanting you to do certain things. There may be room for compromise so both of you can agree on some things. Maybe you still can't stay out to 12 am, but you can come in at 11:00 pm instead of 10:00 pm. It's worth a try. Once they start compromising with you, and you prove to be responsible, you may even get more privileges.

Now every parent is different, so even if you come to them with the greatest plan ever, they still may not budge. However, you can at least try to calmly work out something. What do you have to lose? Start talking!

Dream: Wishing THEY Didn't Do That To You

Hater: The abuse, abandonment, molestation, or neglect that is forever in your mind.

Tip: The one thing I've learned is that buried pain from the past creates future problems when it isn't dealt with. Far too many times young people have confided in me about some awful things that have happened in their lives. I've met people who were molested, abused, assaulted, abandoned, and mistreated in ways that some people could never imagine. But it happened.

The things that happened to these young people were horrible and I wish nobody ever had to experience such things. However the saddest part of the situation was the reactions I would see from them. I saw a lot of anger, disrespect, substance abuse, running away, delinquency, promiscuity, failing grades, etc. They never understood that they were allowing what others did to them ruin their lives. They were simply reacting in the only way they knew how to deal with the painful memories that constantly haunted them. But, they couldn't understand that they still were letting their abusers dictate their world.

As a result of their behaviors, they typically ended up in one of more of the "systems" as I call them. You know the systems (foster care, probation, alternative school, group homes, etc.) None of them enjoyed being a part of any of those "systems", however they had not properly dealt with the painful areas of their past. For that reason, they constantly were in a "system."

A lot of times, young people would share things with me that they wouldn't share with others. That was fine, and I helped them to the best of my abilities, however, some of them needed a lot more help than I could offer. I had to help them understand that it was ok if they talked to someone else. It didn't make them crazy or weak. It actually could help. I would share with them that I had to go talk to a therapist when I experienced a lot of loss in my life. It's no shame in getting help when it's needed. So, I share that same advice with you.

I'm not saying that seeing a therapist, counselor, mentor, case worker, etc. is going to solve all your problems or erase the things that happened in your past. It won't. It takes years for some people to get to a good spot in their lives where the past does not control them any longer. However, I am saying that if you recognize that something in your past is interrupting your life and threatening your chances of a good future, you have to deal with it. Find someone trusted who can help you or get you to the help you need. Your life depends on it.

Bonus Tip: Reporting someone who abused or molested you or someone you know is **NOT** snitching. It is being responsible and hopefully preventing them from ever doing it again. Do the right thing and let someone know right away. If that person doesn't do anything, keep telling until someone does.

Educational Dreams

Education is the key to your future.

I know you've heard a million times how important it is to get an education. Even people who don't really care for school realize the value of education. They know that without certain diplomas, degrees, or certifications, they can't get the jobs and opportunities that they desire. So, getting an education is not an option, it's a requirement.

I've met very few students who had a goal to drop out of high school. Even students I met who had no interest in school still wanted a diploma. They saw the value of an education to their future. I know that you see that same value for yours.

The next few dreams will be about your education and things that go along with it. School comes easily to some people, and for others, it is really hard. Depending on where you fall into those categories is going to determine how you go about achieving your goals. You may have to study hard, or you may learn better through experiential (hands-on) activities. Whatever your style, learn what works best for you and do it.

If you are struggling with some issues in school, it doesn't mean that you will never get it, nor does it mean there is something wrong with you. A lot of people have trouble with school. But those who achieve their dreams find ways around the obstacles.

My advice to you is that you shouldn't try to handle school problems all by yourself all the time. There are people who may be able to assist you and get you through the difficulties. Schools are filled with teachers, counselors, social workers, administrators, etc. to help you. If you don't know who to go to, ask around. You may be surprised who may have been right there to help you all along, if you just ask. People are not mind readers, so you need to let them know, "I need help." Learn to speak up and find the people and things you need. Your future depends on it.

Dream: Avoiding trouble in school

Hater: You are labeled as a trouble maker in school, so regardless of if you did it or not, you get blamed.

Tip: The purpose of school is to educate you, give you a chance to develop critical life skills, and prepare you for your future. That's it. It's your choice what you choose to do with your opportunity.

If you have dreams and goals, a high school diploma is usually the **minimum** for you to accomplish them. So, if you know you need a diploma, why would you skip class? Why do you disrespect teachers? Why do you fight? Why are you failing to complete assignments? Why are you a distraction? I'm confused. If you go to school for an education, then why would you do the opposite?

I know that you don't always like your teachers and administrators. I even know they don't always like you. It's not even about that. It's about you learning what you need to graduate. Simple. Sometimes you have personality clashes with teachers or administrators. Sometimes your teacher rides you so hard because they know you are capable of more, you are just not living up to your potential. Other times there are generational differences.

You feel respect is earned, and your teachers usually feel respect is deserved. Guess what? If you need a grade from them, then you need to try to come to a compromise with them in your communication.

I've worked with students for quite a while now, and the common theme I hear when I ask what causes them problems in school are "teachers and administrators." Usually, it's not all teachers or administrators but certain ones. They feel that they disrespect them, yell at them, pre-judge them, and the list goes on. Well, sometimes those feelings are valid. Then there are times that young people are just placing the blame on everyone else and not accepting responsibility for their actions.

I have personally witnessed adults disrespect, antagonize, and pre-judge young people. So I know it happens. On the other hand, I have also witnessed students who have been blatantly disrespectful to adults. Afterwards they only told what the teacher did. They conveniently left the part where they were disrespectful and uncooperative out. So, I know that wrong can occur on both sides. I will never say that you are wrong because you are a child.

However, you and I both know that as a young person, you tend to get more blame. You get in trouble, not the teacher right?

If you are wrong, own up to your responsibility. School is a lot like your future goals. There will always be people and situations you have to deal with that you'd rather not.   However, you may need those same people to accomplish your goals. So, why not start by practicing your tolerance now? Try holding a conversation with that adult that you really don't get along with (when you both are calm). Or, you can ask your parent or another adult to help you intervene. Even though we don't like to admit it, adults are wrong sometimes.   The suggestions I just gave you are the appropriate ways to handle the situation. Again, this is practice for your future and dealing with uncomfortable situations and people.

Don't place yourself in a losing battle by making things worse for yourself. Face your challenges head on! It's time out for all the craziness if you really want to achieve your dreams.   You are only holding yourself back.   All the unnecessary stuff needs to stop right now. No Excuses!

Dream: Making good grades

Hater: You just can't seem to pass a particular subject.

Tip: You are responsible for your own grades. It's not the teachers fault for going too fast or giving too much work. It's not your classmates who distract you all the time. You are responsible for getting all assignments completed. You are responsible for seeking assistance if you don't understand. You are responsible for giving up a few fun things to make sure you get your work done. So, you have to step up and take ownership for your grades.

If you are struggling, try this. Have a conversation with your teacher about your grades and what you can do to make it better. Ask about tutoring or other extra credit opportunities. Talk to your parents about your struggles and the help you need. SPEAK UP!! Help is available if you just ask (and not the day the assignment is due!)

Now a lot of times, I've found that students don't struggle necessarily because they don't understand, but because they are not prepared. So, let me add some extra tips to this one. I call it the FOCUS method.

1. *Follow All Instructions.* Make sure you read the *entire* assignment and requirements, not just answer the questions you think it asks. It's really easy to mess up an entire assignment just by not reading the instructions correctly. Make sure to ask questions to clarify any tasks you don't understand.

2. *Organization is Important.* You should have a method for keeping track of all your assignments and due dates in one central place. You can put reminders in your phone, computer, notebook, or wherever you choose. The point is that it needs to be somewhere you can see or be reminded regularly.

3. **Complete all assignments entirely.** Whether you feel it's too much work or not, doesn't matter. If you want a good grade, do all the work. Every point you can get helps toward the credit you are trying to earn. I've seen students fail a class by as little as 5 points. Now, if the difference in getting

that five points means completing all the questions on an assignment, isn't it worth it?

4. ***Use your resources fully.*** Nobody expects you to know it all. If you are having trouble, it's no shame in asking for help. Seek out someone who can assist you with completing and understanding your tasks. There are all kinds of assistance available if you speak up, and remember, nobody can read your mind.

5. ***Stay attentive.*** Sometimes you just sit in class and zone out right? It's boring. I know. When am I going to use this in real life? I know. I've felt the exact same way. But, you still need that course credit. Find a way to make it work so you can get the credit and move on!

Dream Hater Activity 3

Educational Success Road Map

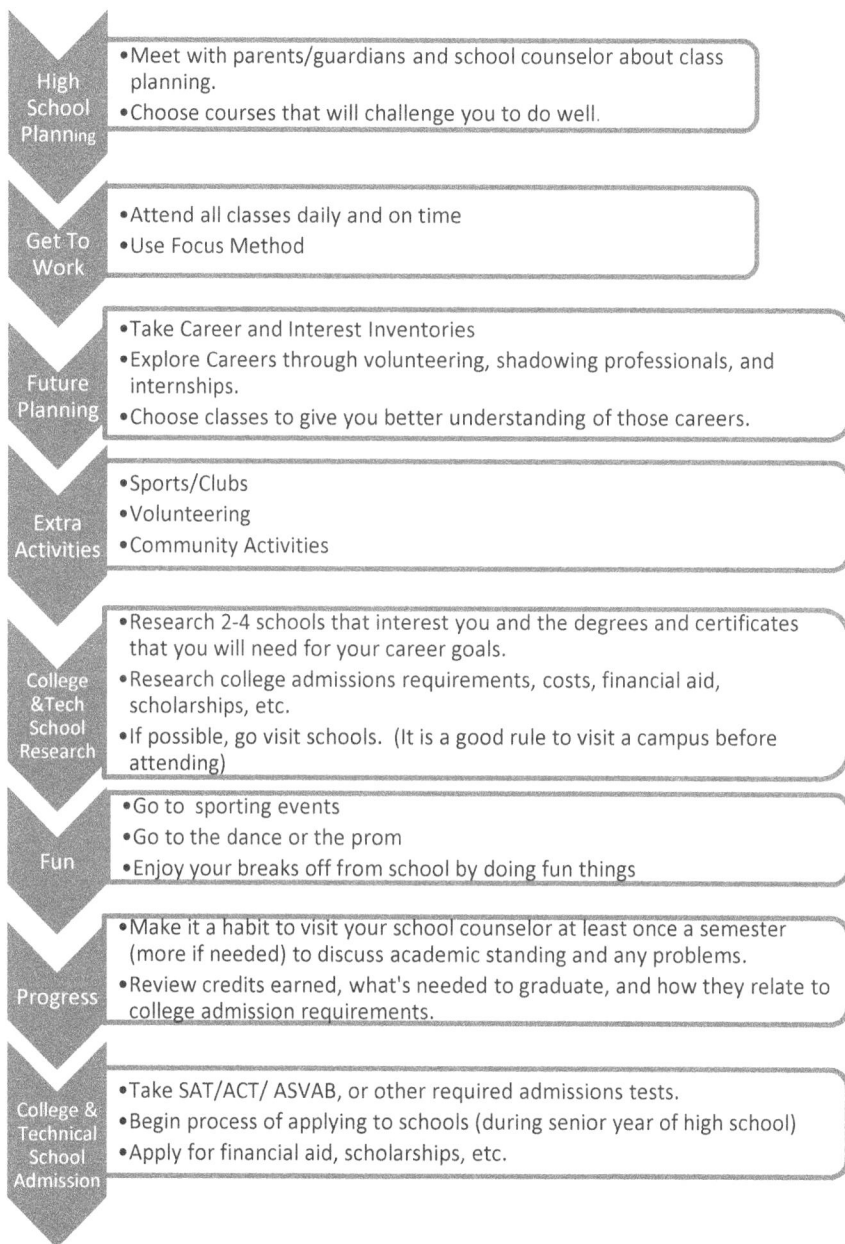

High School Planning
- Meet with parents/guardians and school counselor about class planning.
- Choose courses that will challenge you to do well.

Get To Work
- Attend all classes daily and on time
- Use Focus Method

Future Planning
- Take Career and Interest Inventories
- Explore Careers through volunteering, shadowing professionals, and internships.
- Choose classes to give you better understanding of those careers.

Extra Activities
- Sports/Clubs
- Volunteering
- Community Activities

College &Tech School Research
- Research 2-4 schools that interest you and the degrees and certificates that you will need for your career goals.
- Research college admissions requirements, costs, financial aid, scholarships, etc.
- If possible, go visit schools. (It is a good rule to visit a campus before attending)

Fun
- Go to sporting events
- Go to the dance or the prom
- Enjoy your breaks off from school by doing fun things

Progress
- Make it a habit to visit your school counselor at least once a semester (more if needed) to discuss academic standing and any problems.
- Review credits earned, what's needed to graduate, and how they relate to college admission requirements.

College & Technical School Admission
- Take SAT/ACT/ ASVAB, or other required admissions tests.
- Begin process of applying to schools (during senior year of high school)
- Apply for financial aid, scholarships, etc.

Your success depends on your attitude. A positive attitude equals a positive outcome.

Dream: Graduating from high school

Hater: You have been repeatedly told that you will never graduate.

Tip: The best way to overcome a hater is to make them a liar. So, if your haters have repeatedly tried to beat you down and break your spirit by saying you wouldn't make it; prove them WRONG. It is not too late. I don't care how old you are! If you are still in school and have the opportunity to graduate, then do what you need to do to finish.

If you are too far gone and it looks like you may not be able to graduate the traditional way, you still have the opportunity to go non-traditional routes. There are other ways to graduate. You can try GED programs, technical schools that have GED and trade programs combined, Job Corps, etc. If you don't know how to access these, go online and research what's available to you. Technology makes it very easy to gather information. You typically can find most things you are looking for by using a search engine. You already spend a lot of time online listening to music, watching videos, and social networking. Spend some of that time online doing something that will help you reach your goals. If you

61

still can't find any options, find an adult who may be able to point you in the right direction, as well as hold you accountable to get it done.

I've worked with many students who have had to graduate the non-traditional way. They did not take things seriously in the beginning. They chose to play around and cause trouble instead of focusing on school. So, when they decided they were ready to quit playing and graduate, they were too far behind. It was too late. They had to find alternative methods. Any of them who had to go a different route will tell you how much harder it was to do that, and how they should have taken things seriously when they had a chance. However, despite the obstacles, they got through. So regardless of what's going on, no excuses will do.

It really doesn't matter how you get there, it's just the fact that you GET there! Get moving!

Dream: Continuing your education after high school

Hater: Having to choose between your future and your friends

Tip: As you grow older, you will learn a few things about life and people. Everyone who claims to be your friend does not want you to succeed. It may be jealousy, fear, hatred, or any other reason. Out of all the people you may know and may be cool with today, your life will look very different in about 10 years. There will be some people who will not do anything with their life and will get stuck. So, if they are stuck, do they want to see you do well? Often times they don't. The problem is that regardless of how they feel about you, your plans are very different than theirs. So, how do you handle it?

Everybody is not meant to be in your life forever. As you mature, you will learn that some things about you change. Things you used to like doing may not appeal to you anymore. You develop new habits, interests, and life plans. Sometimes your new interests and the interests of the people around you don't line up.

When I worked with students daily, I would find that on Friday's, they would always want to know what *I* was doing for the weekend. It amazed me that they wanted to know if I was going to the club or do things that mostly appealed to them. I had to explain to them that I had different interests now than I had when I was their age. It didn't necessarily make me old or no fun, I just found fun in other areas. I let them know that I used to like a lot of the same things they did, and still enjoy some similarities, but I was at a different place in life, so I valued and prioritized different things. I learned to be let go of some old habits that did not benefit me anymore.

In order to be successful, you are going to have to let go of some people and habits that are not healthy for you. It doesn't mean that you think you are better than anyone, or more deserving. However, if you have your mind set on a goal, your same old habits are not going to work for you.

Some things about you will have to change. Now, once you decide to change some things for the better, everyone is not going to be down for you. That can be hard, but you will have to keep moving forward. So, if you choose to further your education and your career path, don't feel bad about the success that you will find. You will have earned it.

Some people are going to be left behind. You can try to bring them along, but if they don't want to come, you have to move on. You have to learn to be a little selfish and go get your education. Selfishness is not usually something I promote, but when it comes to your future, you have to think of yourself. Your dreams are too important.

Dream: Making the team

Hater: Despite your hard work and efforts, you still didn't make the team.

Tip: There will be times in life when despite your best efforts, you don't make the team. You work hard, and practice, but you still fall short. As you grow, you will learn that there will be times that you give it your best and you still don't quite get to your goal. I don't want you to think of yourself as a failure. You did your best. It may mean you need to try a little harder, or it may just mean you need to go in a different direction. Understand that whatever is meant for you to do, you will succeed at. It may take you 1000 times to get it right, but you will get there. How can you be a failure if you never stop trying?

While you are still working on making the team, let's talk about attitude. It may be really easy to be upset with the coach, employer, or whoever for not choosing you, or with others who did make the team even though you feel you were just as good or even better. I want you to let that negative attitude go. Everything happens for a reason. Sometimes you don't make the team because it just isn't the right time or fit. It doesn't mean you will never make it, it just means something different needs to take place first.

I don't want you to give up, nor do I want you to have a bad attitude. Congratulate those who did make the team and be a good sport. Think about it, if you had made the team and got a lot of unnecessary attitude from others how would you feel? Your time is coming and when you do get to your goal, you will know you earned it. Remember, sometimes no just means not right now!

Life Dreams

Dreaming about your goals is great. Making them come true is even better.

I'm sure by now you've learned that life can be challenging. Sometimes things you thought would definitely happen didn't; and things you thought would never happen did. Life is a wonderful thing and has lots for you to enjoy. It can also be difficult, but how you choose to handle those obstacles can make all the difference in the world.

The next section covers some common challenges in life. I talk about the struggles, but also talk about the great things that can come. Everyone goes through difficulties at one point or another. The main thing to remember in getting through the difficult times is to keep your words and your attitude in check.

The words you speak have power. Think about it, have you ever known someone who is always negative and speaking crazy things all the time? Don't you absolutely hate being around them? It's because you don't like all the gloom and doom they bring around when they come. It is called negative energy. They live such a miserable life because that is all they talk about! If they turned around their words and outlook, their life would be a lot better. The same goes for you. If you talk about the positive and good things to come, you will have a much better disposition and outlook on life. You will also see those things you want become reality because you spoke it, believed it, and therefore you worked to get it!

A positive attitude is the key to everything you go through in life. It can make or break how successful you become. There will be times where it will be very difficult to keep your attitude in check. When situations occur, we can get angry, irritated, feel defeated, etc. It's hard to keep a positive attitude when you aren't feeling very positive. However, remember that it's just a temporary feeling. You will get past it. Keep a positive attitude that even though things look rough, they won't always be that way. Look forward to that bright future you have ahead of you. You are going to be a huge success!

Dream: Wanting to just do me

Hater: Everyone has something to say about the way I am. This is just me!

Tip: Everyone in this world is an individual. So, while there may be similarities among people, everybody is unique in their own way. I believe that you should always be yourself for YOU, and not for other people.

Individuality is all about being who you are, naturally. You can't be somebody you saw on the street, in a music video, or wherever. It's about who you are on the inside. If you have your own sense of style and interests, nothing is wrong with that. Everyone should be unique in their own way.

Now, one thing that does bother me is when people use the phrase, "This is just the way I am" when referring to your anger, inappropriate dress and language, or other negative things. I do not believe that just because you act a certain way, it is the way you have to stay.

Let me give you an example. Let's say that you are notorious for being the one who ALWAYS goes in on people regardless of your environment or circumstances. Nobody can say anything to you because you aren't having it. They are trying you, and you aren't going to take it!!

I'm not saying this is you, but chances are you know somebody just like this. I know I do. Anyway, the person who goes off without even trying to control themselves has a problem. It's not "just the way they are", it's an excuse. That person uses that as an excuse because they are too lazy to find another way to handle their anger. They constantly create problems and blame others. They are not headed for a great life if they don't figure out how to control their attitude and actions.

Think about it, if I wanted to show up to my office everyday dressed in a t-shirt and jeans (knowing that professional attire is required); what would happen? Or what if every time someone ticked me off, I went IN on them? I'd possibly get sent home to change, or fired because it didn't comply with the rules at my company. I'm an adult, but there are still rules and regulations I have to follow as well if I want certain things in life. I like getting a paycheck, so I have to follow the rules and requirements of my job. Same thing with you, even though you may not care for a rule or people trying to change you into something you are not, you have to comply with the rules.

Your personality and style is just that, yours! Be unique, be an individual, however understand that there are limits on the time and place for you to be yourself however you want to. So, realize that you may have to pull up your pants, watch your language, wear a shirt that is not low cut, or cover up those tattoos. It's not taking away from who you are, it's following rules. We all have to do it, so find a way to handle your business and make it work so that you can keep moving up that ladder of success. Besides, once you prove yourself to be successful on that ladder, nobody ever said you couldn't change the dress code! Think about it!!

Dream: Having what you want, when you want it, and how you want it!

Hater: Regardless of how hard you try, things won't go your way.

Tip: Entitlement is something that many people desire, but very few deserve. Regardless of how you feel, nobody owes you anything. This world is not designed for everyone to get everything they want all the time! It's just not realistic. Now, if you work hard, there is a chance that you can get a lot of things you want, but nobody is going to *give* you anything. The key is hard work and patience. Nothing happens overnight.

I'm not sure why some people seem to feel that life was created to center on them. That is ridiculous. If you are set on taking the "easy" way out and not planning on working for things, you will not reach your dreams. I'll tell you why. Anything you want to do requires hard work. You want to play in the NFL or the NBA? That's a lot of hard work. You want to be the next multi-platinum rapper or singer? That's a lot of hard work. You want to be a chef, doctor, lawyer, engineer, etc.? That's a lot of hard work.

In order to be successful, you have to sacrifice, hustle, and stay on your grind to reach your goals. Nothing comes easy. If it does, it usually won't last long. You know what I mean. That easy street money you see out there. Others make it look really appealing and easy right now. They always have the latest and greatest of everything. But let me tell you something about that lifestyle. People who live like that always have to look over their shoulder and worry about getting caught or hurt. Is that a way to live your life? Who wants to be worried and paranoid all the time?

I like documentaries and "true crime" type shows. There used to be a few different series on about real life gangsters and hustlers. The thing about all of them is that as smart, great, feared, well-known, and even wealthy as some of them were, they all had undesirable consequences as a result of their choices. Many of them ended their careers either in prison or in death. Is that really what you want your legacy to be? Get busy and start your own LEGAL hustle. Yeah, it will be hard work, but you definitely will appreciate the peace of mind that comes from not having to look over your shoulder all the time.

Real friends don't stab you in the back; they have your back!

Dream: Overcoming the bad reputation

Hater: That nasty rumor about you that just won't go away

Tip: Talk is just that, talk. People will talk about anything regardless of any truth that may be present in the conversation. Why do you think tabloids and blogs are so popular? They love to glamorize gossip. Sometimes the stories that others put out are true and sometimes they aren't. Quite a few of them contain partial truths with other parts made up to make the story more interesting.

We all love a good story. Tabloids and blogs have made that a daily part of our lives. We can search for just about anyone's business on the internet. We can also spread a lot of false things and hurt others with the rumors and gossip we put out there. If you were a celebrity, and always had people trying to get in your business, how would you feel? If they made up stories because they really didn't know what was going on, what would you think of that? It happens every day. You may not have to deal with a rumor on an international level like the celebrities do, but it doesn't mean that gossip doesn't hurt you just as much.

So, how do you deal with rumors that hurt you? You remember who you are. I would love for you to understand that what others say about you really doesn't matter, but that takes a long time (if ever) for people to accept. So, in the meantime, how do you get through it?

If the rumors are false, then they usually go away pretty easily. You just have to be strong and endure for a little while. It usually goes away when the next big rumor comes around.

Now if rumors are true, it's a different story. Some people will always hold on to what you used to do and never let you live it down. I know it hurts you and you want to move on. Remember that people who want to continually talk about you and remind you of your shortcomings, ALWAYS have issues of their own. They apparently don't have anything else to do than worry about you, so why spend your time worrying about them? They don't have anything going on for them, so just let it go and move on!

If the rumors continue to go on (true or false), and you are having a hard time dealing with it, don't just deal with it alone. Share it with the support system (family, friends, school staff, etc.) you have so that they can help you through it. Nobody should have to deal with things like gossip and rumors, but if you do, don't just keep it inside.

I do have to say that if you did do something to deserve your bad reputation; you can always make it right. Watch your actions. They speak a lot about your character. If you are ashamed to tell people what you do, then you need to stop doing it. If you say you aren't ashamed, but get upset when people call you out, it still sounds like something you may need to stop doing. Don't make your legacy something you wouldn't want others to know.

Once you stop doing what you *used* to do, focus on moving forward. You can't move forward if you keep looking back. Everyone is entitled to change. Maybe you did make some poor choices and decisions that you are ashamed of. Remember its history, and you don't have to let that hold you down forever. Rise above it and live your life as a changed person!!

There is never a shortage of drama in life. It's all about how you handle it.

Dream: Being able to handle your emotions

Hater: Every time somebody starts with you, you just CAN'T let it go.

Tip: You admit you have issues when it comes to controlling your emotions. You may have difficulties handling your anger, impulses, etc. You may have even been through different self-control groups or even counseling that you didn't really pay attention to because you thought they were whack. So, let's try a crash course in emotion management 101.

Every comment or reaction by a hater does not have to be responded to. I know you feel like if you let it go you are getting punked, and others will want to "try" you. However, you have to know that all that drama isn't worth it every single time. Why waste your energy and time on someone who you don't even like? You have power and control over you, so you should learn to control YOU.

There are plenty of ways to learn how to control you in an unpleasant situation. Some of the most popular ones are counting to 10, removing yourself from the situation, stopping to think before reacting, or finding some way to release your frustration like exercise. The key is finding what works for YOU! Once you learn what calms you down, use it!

In no way am I advocating for you to let people walk all over you and not say anything. I do want you to be successful in asserting yourself when needed, and learning to control yourself as well. The problems occur when you are so upset or angry that you don't think or act rationally.

But, you say you really can't let things go. I know what it feels like to want to go in on someone. I feel that way myself sometimes. However, I can't just go off every time someone upsets me. I wouldn't have a job and I'd probably be in jail. I have to control myself and so do you!

Calming down may be hard for you, but keep trying. Find a place that you can go to when upset and cool down. It may be the local basketball spot, the school counselor's office; a friend's house, or just putting on your earphones and writing. Whatever you do that calms and centers you in the midst of craziness, keep doing it. You will learn how to handle situations much better when you learn to manage the emotion. Learning to control yourself now will make life a lot easier for you later.

Dream Hater Activity 4

Calm it Down

When I'm upset I can calm down by:

1.

2.

3.

4.

5.

I know that controlling my emotions now will help me in my future because:

1.

2.

3.

4.

5.

Dream: Doing "normal teen" things.

Hater: The struggles you have to endure that aren't usually the responsibility of "normal teens".

Tip: So you are accountable for helping to pay bills or take care of family members, or other "adult" responsibilities. However, all you want to do is the go to the football game, the movies, the party, stuff that people your age are supposed to be doing. I feel you. I wish I could take the struggles away and let you live a "normal" life. However, just like that fantasy of being a superhero, I can't take the problems away. I can however, give you some advice.

I used to work with a teen that got into trouble all the time. He was always on 100, just being silly and annoying. He was on the verge of getting put out of school. He really didn't want to get put out, he wanted to graduate. One day we had a one on one moment, and he shared something really profound. He told me that he always acted a fool in school because he had to be serious at home ALL the time. When he got home, he was pressured about paying bills, taking care of younger siblings, and a lot of other things a regular 16 year old shouldn't have to worry about.

Even though it wasn't appropriate, school was his only time to be a kid and just have fun. I gave him this advice, and I'll give it to you as well.

Try this sometimes. Make time for you. See if you can just sneak away and do something you want to do, even if it's only for a few minutes. Everybody needs some down time just to relax or do fun stuff. So, find 30 minutes to go for a walk, a couple of hours to watch a movie, or whatever you like to do. Just make sure you find some time for yourself in the midst of all the work. (Now, don't walk away completely, just take a little break!) You will feel a lot better, and it really may help to keep the stress and pressure down.

Life is not always easy. Some people have more difficult roads to take. However, remember that you have the choice to dwell in your misery and continue to be a victim, or you can fight your way through. While you may get frustrated and tired, you can NOT give up. There is a reason for everything, and this may be the strength you need to build your story. You have read stories or saw movies about people going through problems and then triumphing in the end. Who says that you can't have the same story

one day? Stay strong.

Dream: Not having to go through drama ALL the time

Hater: You work hard to avoid drama, but the drama queen always finds YOU.

Tip: So, you are trying your best to heed my advice. You are trying to do things the right way. You are avoiding drama, controlling your anger, handling your business in school, etc. The problem is that the harder you try to do the right thing, the more drama comes your way.

You really didn't want to get into any mess this year. You wanted to stay away from the rumors, the haters, the arguing, and everything that goes along with all that stuff. Just as soon as you thought you were going to be able to handle it, someone brings drama to your doorstep. So, how you do handle it?

Please understand that there is never a shortage of drama in life. People will continue to try to keep problems going as long as they know you will react to it. If you realize that drama free is the way you want to live, it may be time to change your surroundings.

Changing your surroundings is going to mean changing some of the people you associate with, changing the places you hang out at, and changing your attitude about drama. It is going to be hard, and people who love to keep mess going are going to make it even harder for you. So, you have to make it up in your mind to rise above the drama queen and keep focused on your future. You don't have time for the side show. You have a purpose on this earth, and you have to keep living for it, not the drama!

Sometimes wrong looks so much better than right!!

Dream: Making the right choice

Hater: You know the difference between right and wrong, but wrong looks like so much fun!

Tip: It is not always easy or fun to do the right thing. The wrong thing seems so much more interesting, even when you know the consequences before you do it. I know adults always seem to want to spoil your fun and make it seem like they were never young. They were. And a lot of them did crazy things too. Sometimes that "been there done that" is why they try to keep you away from certain things. Now, how the adults in your life chose to make decisions may be different than you. I don't expect you to always make choices like an adult, because you are not. But, you do know the difference between right and wrong when you are faced with a decision. What you choose to do depends on how important your goals are to you.

So you ask me, "how does going to a party that my parents said I can't go to affect my goals? If I get caught, I'll only get on punishment for a few weeks or have a few privileges taken away." I want you to think a little deeper. Maybe your parents don't want you to go to the party because there won't be proper adult supervision and they are afraid of what could happen. It may be drinking, drugs, X-rated, or other illegal activities going on. Even if you don't participate in those things, being around them can get you in trouble. Imagine if you are up for a scholarship and you get arrested. What if someone has a beef with someone you don't even know and starts shooting? Let's take it even a step further and say what if you drink, smoke, or inhale some lethal mixture and end up dying? I'm just saying. It happens.

Try to make a habit of selecting your friends with similar life goals and interests as you have. When you are faced with difficult choices, you all can be a support system to keep each other encouraged and on the right track. Remember, if you have certain goals, the company you keep can be very important.

I don't want to spoil your fun. Being young is a great time to enjoy life. Just make sure that you can enjoy life, and still not place yourself into crazy situations. It only takes a second to make a choice that can affect the rest of your life. Just stop and think sometimes. You have so much to accomplish. Make sure you get there!

Dream: Wanting to be grown and do whatever you want

Hater: The fact that it seems like forever before you can do certain things **YOUR** way

Tip: I'm sure some adult has told you not to rush to growing up. And you probably said to them that it was easy for them to say. They can do whatever they want to do. They don't have a curfew, anyone to answer to, etc.

Well, the reality is that even adults have certain people to answer to. If they have a job, they have to answer to their employer. If they make money, they pay taxes to the IRS. If they want a house, car, etc. then they have to pay somebody for it. Even if someone decides they want to break the law and end up in jail, they still have to answer to the judge, a guard, probation officer, etc. The point I'm trying to make is that we always have someone to answer to regardless of how old you are.

Also remember that along with age comes more and more responsibility. The older you get, the more you are held accountable for. Think about it. All the luxuries you enjoy, who pays for them? Who pays the rent or mortgage, the electric, and heating bills? The cable and phone bills? Who buys clothes, shoes, and the latest electronics for you?   Someone is responsible for handling all those things and a whole lot more!!

If I could go back to the luxuries of not paying bills and not ALWAYS being responsible all the time, I would jump at the chance. Sure, I enjoy being an adult, and love my life. However, I love where I am now because I enjoyed my life when I was younger. I did things that young people should do when it was time, so now I can be an adult. If I had to be an adult forever, I probably would be over it by now!

I say to you very seriously, don't always rush to be older. You are only going to be young once. Enjoy it. Live your life just as you should for someone who is 14, 15, or 18.   I'm not saying that you should not plan and make preparations for your future, but it's just that, the *future*. Live each day to the fullest. Don't always rush to get to somewhere. If you do, you will miss out on a lot of things that you can enjoy and learn from right now, at the age you are. Slow down, you have a whole life ahead of you!! Besides, who wants to rush to get **OLD**?

Fear is one of the biggest haters you will ever face.

Dream: Wanting to do so many BIG things with your life

Hater: Letting fear keep you from starting or finishing anything

Tip: It's really scary to try something new and take steps towards your dreams. Fear is one of the biggest haters you will ever encounter in your life. Facing fear is a huge task. It is designed to keep people from ever achieving anything.

In order to conquer fear, you have to develop personal strength. Now, I'm not talking about the kind of strength you get from working out and lifting weights. I'm talking about the kind of strength you develop when you have a sense of spirituality or a higher power. Many people use different forms of spirituality to cope. Some people pray, meditate, read or recite daily affirmations, study inspirational books, etc. Whatever your form of spirituality is, you must learn to use it and the power of positive thinking to get you past your fears. When you have a spiritual base, you don't let fear hold you back because you know that you can accomplish anything. Your spirituality keeps you grounded and encouraged even when times are really tough.

If you already have a belief system, I recommend that you become very familiar with it, and learn how to use it to help you through fearful situations. It will really help to empower you and give you a sense of purpose. I live daily by my belief in God. His Word is the one thing that helps me when I feel nothing and nobody else can. It was that belief that enabled me to write this book. Being an author has always been one of my "big dreams" that seemed so far away. But, I prayed and worked and it happened!

If you don't have a form of spirituality, I strongly encourage you to explore one. Research and learn about spirituality. Visit services at a local church, temple, mosque, or other organized form of a belief system. Read books and listen to others. I encourage you to explore and develop your own spirituality for yourself and not base it on the word of others. Many people can mislead you if you aren't aware of what you are doing. So, make it a priority to learn about some higher power and how it can help you overcome the fear in your life.

Dream: Wishing you had the looks of __, the body of__, the money of__, the fame of __, etc.

Hater: Someone always telling you that you don't have what __ has!

Tip: You can only be you. You may not be the object of everyone's desires, or have what someone else does. Worrying about trying to keep up with other people will do one thing for you, wear you out! Trying to be like others will stress you out and keep you from truly being happy. There will always be someone smarter, richer, more attractive, etc. So, you must learn how to be satisfied with who you are.

You can change your weight, hair, eyes, and many other things about your physical appearance. You can work hard, make stacks of money and acquire lots of material things. You can do a lot of things to make yourself more desirable. All of those things can be great.

However, don't let your desired changes make you lose who you are on the inside. Having good looks and money does not make you a good person or someone who others want to be around. Those traits come from inside of you and they can never be bought. It's called character. When you learn who you really are as a person, keeping up with others is not all that important to you. Now, there is nothing wrong with healthy competitions when trying to reach your goals. But, remember, you have to do what makes you happy, not what can defeat someone else.

The internet and reality television have made it incredibly easy to instantly see images of people and groups that have or do things you like. Maybe they have the tattoos, hair, body, clothes, shoes, money, etc. that you want. Nothing is wrong with trying new things and seeing what you like, or even wanting to imitate those things. But, remember to stay true to yourself.

Everyone has a different perception of beauty and success. Learn to accept who you are and develop yourself into an even more wonderful person. Wouldn't we live in a boring world if everyone looked the same, acted the same, and had the same things? Life is interesting because people are all different! That's what makes them unique. So, I dare you to have the nerve to be your own person! You'll be a lot happier being yourself, instead of a carbon copy of someone else!

Dream: Knowing exactly what you want to do with your life.

Hater: Others make you feel crazy because you have no clue as to what kind of career path you plan on taking.

Tip: It is very scary to be expected to plan your entire life at 16, 17, 18, or even 30! Some people are clear on what interests them, and what career path they would like to take early on. Others change their thoughts frequently. Some people don't have a clue as to where to start!

Please be aware that you are not expected to plan out your entire life at such an early age. Things, people, and their interests change. It is not uncommon to find people who start in one career changing to do something totally different years later. So, don't feel bad if you don't know exactly what career path you want to take yet.

When you get ready to go to college, trade, or technical school, it is good to have an idea so that you will have an appropriate major course of study (and not waste money in the process). But, if you have no clue about your path, then how can you choose a major?

There are several ways to learn where your talents and interests lie. You can find online career and interest assessments and inventories that help you to decide what types of things you do and don't like to do. You can make a list of what types of activities you enjoy doing on a regular basis. Another method is to participate in extra-curricular activities at school and volunteer work in the community. By participating in activities, you can learn new things you may have never heard of before. You may learn that you are very good at some things or that you really don't enjoy others. The point is that by doing certain activities and tasks, you start to learn what your particular interests and dislikes are. This works even for people who do know what they want to do. Sometimes when people actually start working in a field, they find that they really don't like it. Save some time and energy by volunteering first.

I challenge you to do this activity to help you learn your skills and interests. Find a club at school or a community agency that you normally would not participate in. Get involved if only for one activity. You may be surprised and learn something about yourself and your interests.

Dream: Wishing that EVERYONE would get out of your business.

Hater: EVERYONE is always in your face about something.

Tip: Don't you just get tired of everyone always being in your business about something? It could be your parents, relatives, teachers, or any adult that always has some say about what you have going on. Regardless of who it is, you get tired of everyone else having a say about your life.

Let's work through this one.   People who have your best interest at heart want to see you do well. Yeah, sometimes they go overboard and you really could do without the nagging and advice you never asked for. However, they really want you to succeed in life and they really feel like they are helping (whether they are or not).   I suggest that you just give them a chance and listen to what they have to say. You may or may not take their advice, but it's worth hearing. While listening, it's possible that you may learn something you really did need to know.

I'll tell you another reason you should listen. Sometimes it's easier to suck it up and listen to what they have to say now, rather than have people in your business that you really don't want there. What kind of people? I'm talking about law enforcement, judges, probation officers, mandatory counselors, etc. If you never listen to others and just do everything you want to do, chances are that there will be a bunch of strangers that you never wanted all in your business!

Nobody knows everything. We should all listen and learn from others sometimes. Besides, you really may learn something to help you on your path. So, sit down and just listen. Sometimes those people all up in your business are the ones who will help you get some business of your own!!

Time for Action

I dare you to be your own person!

You are stronger than you know and can handle a lot more than you think. I said that to let you know that it's not a matter of *if,* it's *when* the haters will come. Now, that's not to say that you should live your life in fear or worrying about things going wrong. Remember, WE don't live in fear any longer right?

I just want you to understand that even though you may try your best, and follow all the "rules", sometimes haters will still try find a way to destroy you. Haters come in many forms. They can come in the form of racism, gender and sexual orientation discrimination, negative people, and in many other ways. There is not enough paper and ink for me to even begin to explain how to deal with some of those haters because I still struggle with some of those issues myself. I have personally experienced discrimination as a black person, as a woman, and as someone who did not fit the "mold" that was established. I will be the first to admit that I have been angry, hurt, and amazed at the ignorance of some people. However, I do know that focusing on God and staying on the grind He set for me has made overcoming my own haters a lot easier to deal with. I remember that HE is the one who gets me through everything. So, even though I have dealt with my own roadblocks, I know that I still have purpose, and I'm still important. I enjoy life, and live it to its fullest. My hope is that you learn how to do the same.

I talked a lot about ways to overcome your haters. However, once you overcome them, you still have a lot of work to do. So, I want to leave you with a few tips for reaching those goals you have.

1. Discover your interests and then research them

If you could do just one thing every day, what would it be? What are you good at? What do you like doing? What sparks your interest that has stayed with you for a while? Start paying attention to those things, and then start researching them for your future.

I never understood how young people could tell me that they wanted to be a doctor, but they don't like science and they are currently failing all of their high school classes. You have to learn to do your research and learn what is realistic and what is practical for your future.

For example, if you want to be in the music industry, then I expect that you will do more than write lyrics and rap. You need to learn about trends, executive duties, business aspects, marketing, public relations, image, etc. Have you ever watched the television documentary shows and see how all of these great, talented musicians and artists are now broke? Achieving your dream only to have a hater snatch is from you is not cool. That's why you have to learn or at least be aware of EVERYTHING!! (Remember that next time you ask when are you going to use this in real life?) There is so much more to your dreams than you realize. The people who really get to "live their dreams" put a lot into researching and learning everything they need to know about their goals.

2. Put your plan in writing

Put everything you want to do down on paper. Don't just keep it in your head. Use that written plan as a roadmap to guide you. When you get off track, just pick it up and get back on course. It's ideal to put it somewhere you will see it often to keep you reminded why you are working so hard.

Everyone has their own method for how they write down their dreams. Some people make collages or vision boards. Some people keep a notebook or journal. Some people keep their things in their phone, on their computer, tablet, or some other electronic method. Choose whatever works best for you. I simply want you to write it down and look at it often as a way to keep you focused on what you are supposed to be working for. It helps sometimes when things get hard, and you are tempted to give up. When you look at that paper or whatever, it reminds you that you are doing it all for a reason!

3. Stay focused

Don't let meaningless things distract you. A lot of things that you let get in your way have no importance to your future. So, don't give them your time. If you mess up, and fall off course, it's ok. Everyone makes mistakes. The important thing to remember is that you have to get back on track. When you stay off track is when it's NOT ok.

A big part of staying focused is diligence. You keep working daily on what you want. Think of it this way. Olympic athletes are the best at what they do. They go on to win numerous competitions resulting in medals and other awards. Do you think they got to that level without hard work? Of course not! Do you think they got distracted? Of course at times, but the difference was that they got back on track because they knew they were destined for greatness. You are destined for that same greatness, but you have to keep your focus on what motivates you.

4. Choose your friends and associates carefully

Just because someone smiles at you does not make them your friend! Remember, everyone you encounter may not be in your best interest. Watch out for fake friends or haters in disguise. How can you tell the difference in fake and real friends?

Fake Friends

Repeatedly tell you that you can't

Put you in bad or dangerous situations

Throw you off track often

Are never around when things aren't going so well

Real Friends

Tell you that you can, and you WILL

Never place you in bad situations, and usually try to keep you out of them

Help you stay on track by being honest, even when you don't like what they say

Are always around when times are hard

Of course you can add more things to the short lists I just gave. However, you get the idea. Keep your eyes and ears open so you know how to deal with the different people you will encounter.

5. Chase your own dreams

You have to be yourself. You cannot live out anyone else's dream but your own. It's great to work with someone who has the same ideals and goals as you because together, you can do twice as much. However, don't attach to other people's dreams just because it sounds like a good idea. If it's not in your heart, it won't work. Remember, you are unique, and can only do YOU!!

6. Work hard

Nothing worth having is easy to come by. You can't be lazy and expect your dreams to fall out of the sky. In order to reach your goals, you are going to have to put in real work and stay on the grind. Also, remember, you may have to start low, but it's just that a start. Don't be too good to do the ground work until you can work your way up. There are a lot of people who started at the bottom, but didn't stay there. Think of it this way, if you start at the bottom, you have two choices. You can either stay there, or work hard to move up from the bottom. What happens is totally up to how bad you want it.

7. Be responsible

Own up to your mistakes and work to make them right. Apologize when you are wrong. Learn to control yourself even when things are difficult. Remember that blaming others never solves issues. Even if others are causing problems for you, keep in mind that you can only control you!! Keep a positive attitude in all situations.

Another part of being responsible is adhering to a set of personal standards. Don't just go with the flow and accept anything. Maintain your values and stay true to your beliefs. Do the right thing even if everyone around you chooses not to.

8. Develop a relationship with a higher power

Stay grounded with your spirituality. Develop a strong relationship with your higher power. It will be the constant that will take you through even the most challenging things in life. Your spirituality can help you make your way through challenging times by having that supreme authority to trust in. If you don't have a higher power, I strongly suggest you find one soon!

Think about it. On award shows, who are the two most thanked? God and mama right? Winners know where their strength comes from. Shouldn't you?

9. Never stop dreaming

You can never give up on those dreams you have. Even if you planned on being a millionaire by 30, and find that you are only a hundredaire at 30, keep working at it.

Nobody has you on a time table but you. You will get there!

10. NO EXCUSES

Those two words, NO EXCUSES, are the most important piece of advice I can give you. I don't care what kind of crazy messed up things come your way, you've got work to do and you can't let the haters keep you from your goals.

No more saying why you can't, or how hard it is, or how much work it is, or ANY excuse at all. There is an anonymous quote that begins, "Excuses are meaningless tools of the incompetent." So, let go of all the reasons it didn't happen and either find a way or make a way for it to happen. All excuses for not working towards your goals are null and void from this moment forward!

I'm going to restate # 10 in case you missed it. NO EXCUSES!! Excuses are not acceptable. You are only limiting yourself with all the negative talk about why you can't do something. Start putting it out there that you CAN do things!! A positive attitude goes a long way when you start reaching for your goals.

I know this book sounds like I'm trying to hype you up about your future. You know what? I AM!! You have so much to look forward to, and I want to see you reach every dream you have for yourself. There are so many things to do, places to see, and people to meet in this world. Make sure you take advantage of all life offers you. You only live once, make it count!

I can't wait to see what you do!! I know you'll be great at it!!

Dream Hater Activity 5

Hater Action Plan

1. **Set a Goal**: (Based on likes, or areas of interest)
   Ex. I want to become a ... or I want to start doing…..

   A. _____

   B. _____

   C. _____

2. **Avoid distractions** (People, places, or things that will throw you off track. Be honest!)
   Ex. I will avoid associating with…or in the area known for…..

   A. _____

   B. _____

   C. _____

3. **Set a plan for dealing with haters** (Be prepared for them)
   Ex. When I am confronted with _____, I will _____.

   A. _____

   B. _____

   C. _____

4. **Stay positive**. (Even when things go wrong, keep your head up.)
   Ex. When I am feeling down, I will ………..

   A. _____

   B. _____

   C. _____

Appendices

Resources

Free On-Line Educational Resources, Career, and College Planning

http://www.educationplanner.org

http://www.myfuture.com

http://www.driveofyourlife.org

http://www.college-visits.com

http://www.mybetedu.com

http://public.careercruising.com/us/en/

http://jobstar.org/tools/career/spec-car.php

http://mappingyourfuture.org/

https://bigfuture.collegeboard.org/

http://www.todaysmilitary.com/

http://www.jobcorps.gov

http://www.gedtestingservice.com

https://www.ngycp.org/site/

Hotlines, Help lines, and Resources

http://www.thehotline.org (Domestic Violence Hotline) 1-800-799- SAFE (7233)

http://www.findtreatment.samhsa.gov (Mental Health and Substance Abuse)

http://www.1800runaway.org/ (National Runaway Switchboard)

www.suicidepreventionlifeline.org (Suicide Prevention Life Line) 1-800-273-TALK (8255)

Local Resources

Use your local resources! School, church, and community members

Epilogue

I would love to hear from you. The good, the bad, and the ugly. If you have feedback or suggestions, need to find help in your area with something, or just want to share your dreams and challenges. I want to hear from you!! I will try my best to get back with you as soon as I can! Twitter @terarreid or via my website, www.terareid.com.

Tera

Acknowledgements

First and foremost, I want to give a huge thanks to the Almighty God for his unconditional love and enduring grace. Without Him, I would have never been able to complete this task.

For over 20 years Kim Roberson has been someone I could always count on to be in my corner. Thanks for the feedback, editing, financial, and ongoing emotional support. Love you girl!

To my "Atlanta mama", Carolyn Freeman, thank you for your editing support, feedback, and encouragement. You are so special!

A huge thanks goes to those who contributed to my campaign to fund this project. Pastor Kevin & Patryce Harvey, I love you guys! Keisha Graham, thanks for being in my corner girl! Priscilla & Dennis Brown, your support means so much to me! Thanks again!!

I also want to shout out those who helped me in some aspect of learning how to get my thoughts out to the world and into print. William Smith, Travis Hunter, Stephanie Stafford, and Teresa Hardy, I appreciate all the resources and direction pointing.

Thank you to my wonderful and patient designer, graphic artist Jeff Crosby at Scorpio Soul Designs. You are the best!!

To all my family and friends who often would check on me and offer support, this is for you as well. I can't possibly name everyone, but know that you helped this dream come true. Love you all!

To my father, Willie Reid, Sr., my grandparents, and other relatives who have gone on to Heaven, but not before leaving their mark on my life, this book is for you also. I love and miss you all.

Lastly, I want to thank my biggest cheerleader for my entire life, my mother, Lottie Reid. I'm proud to call you mom and thank you for all you've done for me! I hope I've made you proud. I love you.

About the Author

Tera R. Reid, known as "Ms. Reid" to young people throughout the southeast is a social worker who has advocated for young people for over 18 years. She has become as an expert on conquering the unique challenges faced by young adults and their families by providing practical, realistic solutions to every day stressors.

Tera is a sought after speaker, trainer, consultant, and author on a variety of young adult topics ranging from adolescent, parenting, and community issues. She is also the CEO of Transforming Other's Potential, Inc., an agency that provides mentoring opportunities to teens and provides professional development to those serving young people.

Ms. Reid is a proud graduate of North Carolina A&T State University with a Bachelor of Social Work degree, and Clark Atlanta University with a Master of Social Work degree.

Tera believes in the Proverb, "To whom much is given, much is required". She lives by this motto as she strives to help others reach their goals.

Disclaimer

This book is designed to provide advice and guidance on ways to handle unpleasant situations that may arise in daily living. It is sold with the understanding that the publisher and author are not engaged in rendering legal, therapeutic, educational, or other professional services. If legal, therapeutic, or educational assistance is required, the services of a competent professional should be sought.

It is not the purpose of this book to be a substitute for any professional services needed, but instead to complement, amplify, and supplement those services. You are urged to seek professional assistance as much as possible to address your individual needs.

Every effort has been made to make this manual as complete and accurate as possible. However, there may be mistakes, both typographical and in content. Therefore this text should be used only as a general guide and not as the ultimate source of information and assistance. Furthermore this book contains information that is only current up to the printing date.

The purpose of the book is to educate, entertain, and inspire. The author and publisher shall have neither liability nor responsibility to any person or entity with respect to any loss or damage caused, or alleged to have been caused, directly or indirectly, by the information contained in this book.

www.ingramcontent.com/pod-product-compliance
Lightning Source LLC
Chambersburg PA
CBHW072028040426
42447CB00009B/1775